The Sabbath

A DAY OF DELIGHT

by Sophia N. Cedarbaum
Pictures by Clare & John Ross

Union of American Hebrew Congregations

Sabbath Evening

DEBBIE and Danny hurry home from school on Friday afternoon.

They have much to do before the Sabbath begins.

The Sabbath is a very special day.

The Sabbath is a day of rest—of joy—and of fun.

The Sabbath begins on Friday at sundown.

Debbie and Danny help set the table for dinner.

They know where to place the gleaming Sabbath candlesticks, the wine bottle, the shin-

ing silver kiddush cups, and the chalo under
its pretty cover.

The Sabbath meal is like a dinner party.

Often there are guests. Debbie and
Danny are happy when cousins, aunts and
uncles, or friends come for Sabbath dinner.

Father says the Sabbath is like a pretty
bride or queen. He invites the guests to be
seated. "Come," he says, "let us welcome the
Sabbath in joy and peace."

Mother recites the blessing over the
lighted candles:

BORUCH ATO ADONOY ELOHENU MEL-
ECH HO-OLOM ASHER KID'SHONU
B'MITSVOSOV V'TSIVONU L'HADLIK
NER SHEL SHABOS.

BLESSED ARE YOU, O LORD OUR GOD,
KING OF THE WORLD, WHO MADE US
HOLY BY YOUR COMMANDMENTS AND

COMMANDED US TO KINDLE THE SAB-
BATH LIGHT.

Father raises his kiddush cup and says,
"Let us praise God with this symbol of joy
and thank Him for the blessings of the past
week."

Danny recites the first part of the Kiddush:

BORUCH ATO ADONOY ELOHENU MEL-
ECH HO-OLOM BO-RE P'RI HAGOFEN.

BLESSED ARE YOU, O LORD OUR GOD,
KING OF THE WORLD, WHO CREATES
THE FRUIT OF THE VINE.

They all sip their wine.

Debbie lifts the chalo cover and says the
blessing over the bread:

BORUCH ATO ADONOY ELOHENU MEL-
ECH HO-OLOM HA-MOTSI LECHEM
MIN HO-ORETS.

BLESSED ARE YOU, O LORD OUR GOD,
KING OF THE WORLD, WHO BRINGS
FORTH BREAD FROM THE EARTH.

Father slices the chalo and passes pieces to all the guests.

"Shabbat shalom," cry Debbie and Danny.

"Shabbat shalom—a peaceful Sabbath," reply their mother and father and all the guests.

After dinner no one is in a hurry to leave the table. Debbie brings out the song books and they sing z'miros. These are Sabbath songs.

They sing songs in English and some in Hebrew. Father starts off with "Shalom Aleichem."

Debbie's favorite is "Sabbath Queen."

The sun on the tree-tops
    no longer is seen;

Come, gather to welcome
    the Sabbath, our Queen.
The Sabbath is coming,
    the holy, the blest,
And with her good angels
    of peace and of rest.
Come here, come near,
    and here abide,
Welcome, welcome,
    dear Sabbath Bride.
Peace also to you, O angels
    of peace.

Danny likes *Tzur Mishelo,* "Rock of Plenty."

The last song they sing is really a prayer. It is called "Grace." It thanks God for their food.

BORUCH ATO ADONOY, HAZON
ES HAKOL.

BLESSED ARE YOU, O LORD,
WHO PROVIDES FOOD FOR ALL.

Services

DEBBIE and Danny always go with their mother and father to the Family Services at their temple.

As they arrive at the temple they hear the organ playing softly.

In the lobby people greet each other with "Good Shabos" or "Shabbat shalom."

They enter the synagogue and find their seats quickly.

Debbie and Danny enjoy the hushed feeling of the synagogue.

The Ner Tomid, the Eternal Light, hanging over the Holy Ark, seems to twinkle a special welcome to them.

The tall seven-branched m'noros, standing one at either end of the pulpit, look cheerful and bright.

There are pretty flowers on the pulpit.

Everything seems to glow and say, "Sit back. Be comfortable. This is the time to think of pleasant and good things."

The rabbi begins the service with a short prayer.

The boys and girls of the religious school choir sing the opening hymn. They look very pretty in their blue robes with white collars.

The rabbi asks the congregation to open their prayer books. The rabbi reads from the prayer book. It is like a poem.

The congregation joins in the *Bor'chu* and the *Sh'ma*.

The congregation also joins in the singing.

The cantor sings the Kiddush. The congregation sings with him.

The rabbi's sermon is a story. The rabbi is a good story teller. Everyone listens very carefully.

The children who have birthdays this month receive a special honor. They are invited to come up to the pulpit. The rabbi blesses each birthday child. Debbie and Danny watch to see which of their friends has a birthday. They look forward to the time when it will be their turn to be blessed.

After the closing hymn the rabbi blesses the congregation. The service is over.

Once again Debbie and Danny and their parents wish each other "Shabbat shalom." Everyone else in the congregation turns to his neighbor and his friends to wish them "Shabbat shalom."

Sabbath Morning

DEBBIE and Danny enjoy going to Sabbath morning services.

In their temple boys and girls are sometimes called upon to read part of the service. Some are asked to say the blessings before and after the reading of the Torah.

The high point of the service comes when the Holy Ark is opened. The Torah scrolls are kept in the Ark.

When the Ark is opened the congregation stands.

The rabbi takes the Torah from the Ark. Facing the congregation, he holds the Torah high and leads them in reciting the Sh'ma:

SH'MA YISROEL ADONOY ELOHENU,
ADONOY ECHOD.

HEAR, O ISRAEL, THE LORD, OUR GOD,
THE LORD IS ONE.

Once in a while the rabbi leads a Torah procession. He carries a Torah around the aisles of the synagogue.

Debbie and Danny stand where they can get a good view of the Torah. It has a lovely velvet cover. It has beautiful decorations, a silver crown and a silver breastplate. Debbie and Danny are very quiet and listen carefully. Now they can hear the sound of the tiny bells on the Torah crowns.

A silver pointer shaped like a little hand hangs from the Torah. It is called the "yod." The rabbi uses it when he reads from the Torah.

Before he reads from the Torah the rabbi takes the silver ornaments and the cover off the Torah. He lays the Torah down on the reading desk. He unrolls the Torah and reads from it about God and the Jewish people.

Sabbath afternoon

SABBATH afternoon is the time to have fun with family and friends. It is a time to do something especially pleasant.

Very often Debbie and Danny and their friends have a party called an *Oneg Shabbat* —a Sabbath delight.

Sometimes they take a walk in the park with their mother and father.

Best of all they like to visit their grandparents. Grandmother is sure to have plenty of her special crisp sugar cookies on hand. She loves to read from the Bible.

Grandfather can always be teased into telling wonderful stories of when he was a boy.

When they go home they have fun pretending they are grandmother and grandfather. They play that they have grandchildren and they tell them about all the fun that they had on Shabbat.

In the Evening

AS THE day begins to fade Debbie and Danny help their mother prepare for Havdolo.

Their family loves to celebrate it. They bring a tall cup of wine, the spice-box filled with all kinds of sweet-smelling spices, and the braided Havdolo candle.

Father lifts the cup of wine and says, "O Lord, our God, at this twilight hour we gather to thank You once more for the joys of the Sabbath which we have known in happy family union."

Danny chants the blessing over the wine.

Debbie recites the blessing over the spices. She smells the lovely fragrance and passes the spice-box around to the family.

Debbie holds the braided candle while Father recites the blessing for the light.

Debbie and Danny and their parents are thankful for the Sabbath and its beauty. Now they are ready for the week's work.

They greet the new week with the song,
"Shovua Tov":

A good week, a week of peace,

May gladness reign and joy increase.

A good week, a week of peace,

May gladness reign and joy increase.

SHOVUA TOV!

May you, too, have a good week.